T0063002

Abbi's
Forever Home

A Memoir For Two

Elizabeth Cooke

abbott press

Abbott Press books may be ordered through booksellers or by contacting:

Abbott Press
1663 Liberty Drive
Bloomington, IN 47403
www.abbottpress.com
Phone: 1 (866) 697-5310

ISBN: 978-1-4582-2166-7 (sc)
ISBN: 978-1-4582-2165-0 (e)

Library of Congress Control Number: 2018903192

Print information available on the last page.

Abbott Press rev. date: 03/15/2018

Chapter One

MY FOREVER HOME

Although this volume is a memoir for two, I am really putting it together for both of us. My name is Abbi.

I first came to HER house only a few weeks ago, but we bonded on sight. All I know is that from now on, SHE is my person, and that I am oh so lucky to have HER.

SHE is a 92–year-old woman named Elizabeth. SHE has a bad left eye, scratchy skin, and only seven teeth of HER very own.

I am an equally old (in dog years) toy poodle that has lost my right eye, has scratchy skin and also seven teeth. The two of us are now soul mates, sisters under that scratchy skin. Together, as one – with my good left eye and HER good right one – we manage to get the whole picture.

In HER earlier life, people said SHE was something of a *femme fatale*, a woman of mystery. At least, that's what SHE tells me.

SHE also says the only mystery, as far as SHE is concerned, is HERSELF.

Mystery number one: Why did SHE have three husbands?

Well, I've had a few myself – in the puppy mill. Ugh!

Mystery number two: Why, as a liberal democrat, did SHE end up near Atlanta, Georgia, a conservative area of the United States?

I wasn't born in Georgia either. Don't know where. Somewhere up North, I think, surely a more liberal place than here.

Mystery number three: Incidents, coincidence, and dumb luck.

The biggest dumb luck, of course, is mine, coming to live with HER, being able to talk to HER. SHE feels my story and knows my early miseries better than anyone ever has because nobody ever bothered to know.

And I know HERS because I want to.

When I first arrived here, I was pretty disoriented. I had been living in a foster home, with several other dogs – one with a missing paw, another with only three legs – and of course, I fit right in, being blind in one eye. Fortunately, my good eye is 20/20.

HER house is so different from the foster home, which naturally was far better than the awful shelter cage I was in before I was fostered. At the shelter, I got such fleas that I lost all the hair on my backside. The food was pretty bad – a kind of mush– and my teeth were rotten.

When I was saved by the fostering group, first I had a spay operation, then I had medicinal baths for my flea infestation that got rid of the little buggers. Next, they operated on my bad eye, closing it permanently. Finally all my rotten teeth were removed, leaving seven, including the two front fangs (so I can chew).

"God, Abbi, you have dragon breath," my foster mother told me, before the teeth extractions. Now, my mouth smells of roses – or perhaps, what I have just eaten. My foster mother also told me that the awful shelter people were going to put me down.

"You were due to be euthanized, Abbi. But we got you just in time."

I don't know that big word, but I get the idea. I missed a bullet!

I am saved! Now life is so different. I am getting used to my forever home as each day goes by. SHE is really good to me. The food I get? Delicious! The treats SHE gives me? Superior! SHE even bought me a little bed of my own with its pillow and a fox toy to chew on. I use the bed, which SHE put up on the red sofa beside HER when SHE is reading the newspaper. Mostly – and of course, every night – I sleep next to HER in the crook of HER arm – even during an afternoon nap - in HER own big bed. We snuggle.

I know SHE loves me.

That's the best part of it all. SHE is my person. I am the heartbeat in HER house. SHE lives alone. I have always lived alone, but no longer.

We talk together. It's a different kind of language, exchanged through touch, through eye contact, through my occasional yap, or a fake growl, which I pull from time to time (always with my cropped tail wagging), just to make sure SHE is listening.

That is why I put together this book, to let you know, as we get old, what beauty there is between HER and me, and the wisdom we each impart to one another. We come from a parallel universe, our pasts somehow conjoined.

I am told not even a husband or a wife or a son or a daughter could have the same bond as a dog and her (or his) person. Man's (or woman's) best friend? I know it's trite. In fact, for the two of us it's more than just friendship. As I said in the beginning, we are sisters under the skin (scratchy) but mostly in the heart.

SHE and Abbi...what a team!

Chapter Two

OLD

I am glad we are both old. SHE has a few more years on HER than I have on me. All I know is we both need a lot of sleep. Also, we each have aches and pains but somehow they mesh and we hurt together.

"Abbi, you're my inspiration!" SHE will exclaim. "When I pet you, my blood pressure goes down."

This makes me happy. Nobody ever really wanted me – until now. SHE does. I can feel it. The fostering group that saved my life is really excited by my finding my forever home. They never thought it would happen.

Neither did I!

And here I am. Lucky me. In the evening, we sit together on the red couch in the living room, me in my small bed next to HER, SHE on the cushions by my side. They say animals don't see color, but I certainly see that bright red couch. Hah! What about the bull in the bullring? He sure sees the red cape!

I love my bed on the couch. It just fits me. It has its pillow and a blanket – so soft. I know SHE bought it to match me. I am flattered. I am what they call an apricot toy poodle, not that I'm really apricot color. My fur is sort of a yellowish gray, same as my bed.

It's the first time I ever owned anything, that something is actually mine.

Sometimes, SHE will lean over and gently blow on my face.

"Do you like vodka, Abbi?" SHE will say with a smile.

I wrinkle my nose. SHE will have only the one drink. It's tall – unless HER son, his wife, and the grandchildren come over for a small party. This happens frequently. The kids always treat me with great affection. I reciprocate.

They are all good to me, except for the great granddaughter, Clare. At two years old, she's a real handful. It's true what they say about the 'terrible twos'! I attest to that. She pats me too hard, pulls my ears, screeches at me, until one of her parents, usually her Daddy, Daniel, (HER grandson) pulls Clare away. Whew! What a relief.

HER granddaughter, Evie, is more my age – about 11 years old, (in human years) I would think. Evie lies on the floor next to me, and whispers "Abbi, Abbi, Abbi" and kisses my nose. What a sweet girl. I give her a little lick back.

"Did you know it was me who found you? I did! I saw your picture on PetFinder on the computer and thought you'd be perfect for my grandma…who I knew was lonely for a dog. And look what happened. You are here, Abbi, and you are perfect, a match made in heaven."

I lick Evie all the harder. I have a family!

"I knew grandma and you were made for each other. Look at your whiskery face and your funny little teeth."

I don't have funny teeth.

"You and grandma each have a funny smile."

Evie's grandma and I look alike? I'm flattered.

Evie laughs. The little girl understands me because she says, "in a way, you know, you really do."

SHE uses the computer a lot. One day, SHE was busily Googling something. I couldn't see what, but I heard HER exclaim, "It's enough to make me sick! How can people be so cruel – litter after litter – to sell to pet stores…for the money!"

I realized SHE was learning about puppy mills.

"When the female is worn out, she's discarded, thrown onto the heap of carcasses back of the puppy mill property – a mass grave! I can't believe this."

SHE shuts the computer off in disgust. I could see there are tears in HER eyes. I come over and give HER a lick on the hand.

SHE looks at me. "How many puppies did you have, sweet Abbi?"

I shake my head, which makes my ears fly. I really don't know. I never counted. I had puppies – four or five at a time – every few months. I used to clean them, suckle them, take a sniff of each one – kind of a head count – Then in a few weeks, after weaning them, they'd all be gone.

In the beginning, when this happened, when I was a young dog, it was sad because I cared about them. It was a misery. It tugged at my heartstrings to lose them, but as it happened so often – so always – I forgot to count and that made me forget to care. I just couldn't anymore.

SHE leans down to pat me. "Such a big heart in such a small package," SHE whispers.

I was licking my front paws.

"Why do you keep licking those feet?" SHE asks. "Lick, lick, lick." SHE looks at my paws carefully. They have tiny scars. "Poor little Abbi," SHE says. "I used to bite my nails."

I wondered why. Had SHE been in a kind of cage?

I didn't want to tell HER that when I lived in a stacked cage at the puppy mill, the floor of the cage was just the same old wire. There was no actual floor. The wire began to hurt my paws, bit into them. Sometimes, they were bloody. I knew this knowledge would only make her hate puppy mills more, but maybe that would be a good thing.

What kind of cage could SHE have lived in that made HER bite HER nails? This bothered me. I could not get it out of my head.

The end of that puppy mill finally happened when the health department came and closed it down. Neighbors had complained of the stench in the woods behind the building, particularly in the summer heat. It came from the open grave at the back of the property under the trees, where the discarded dogs lay – out in the open, in the midst of buzzing flies.

It was a blessing for me. I was going on eight years old, over the limit, and knew my time was coming. I was saved by the health department and put into a regular shelter.

It was a better place. The cage was ground level and at least had a floor made of dirt. We also got to play on some grass outside for an hour every day. The food was – okay, I guess, not great - but better than the slop at the puppy mill. I was there until three days before I was due to be put down. My foster parent arrived and took 10 of us home with her and her husband.

They had a big back yard. What a reprieve! And the kibble – which my foster mother warmed to soften it (my teeth, you know – or lack of) before she gave it to me, was better than any food I ever had. My foster parents were good to me.

But now, I am in a different world. Now, SHE spoils me rotten. Oh what bliss!

"Hungry, little Abbi?" SHE will tease me at breakfast – around 7:00 AM, or dinnertime, around 5:30.

I jump with anticipation. What I eat at HER house is *gourmet!* SHE bought for me little trays of dog food with chicken flavor, *filet mignon* flavor – and these SHE puts on top of the softened kibble.

"Bon appetit!" SHE will exclaim, placing my dish on the floor of the laundry room.

I guess these are French words. SHE tells me how SHE loves Paris, that SHE lived there, was in love there for three whole years when SHE was in her twenties.

One day, SHE decided to cook a cheese *soufflé*.

"Abbi, don't get under my feet, little dog," SHE exclaims as SHE is whipping egg whites. "Did you know I went to the *Cordon Bleu* when I was in Paris?"

I love the way SHE talks to me.

"It was a six weeks course. You went everyday, all day – like at school. Well, it was a school. The head chef looked like Santa Claus, wore a white chef's hat and had a wooden leg. And he was tough." SHE was combining the egg whites with the yellow yolk concoction.

As SHE placed the dish into the hot oven, SHE continued, "Best way to learn the language. When you're holding a hot, sizzling pan, the words just come to you. You learn French fast because you have to."

Later, when the puffy concoction emerged from the oven, SHE sat down to a portion SHE put on a plate.

"Oh, this is good…so cheesy…so light." In a spoon, SHE scooped a small dollop. "I'm going to let this cool, Abbi. Then you can have a taste." Soon enough, I was able to devour the spoonful in one quick bite. It was *formidable!*

Even I was learning French.

This, of course, is not the only special tasting SHE allows me. I get all sorts of delicate treats, a bit of white meat chicken, a morsel of piecrust, a tiny portion of scrambled egg. It's all okay – so far - because I still weigh only nine pounds.

We'll see how long that lasts!

Chapter Three

CAGE

I still wonder if SHE was in a cage, else why would SHE bite her nails? Do people have cages? – maybe, in a prison, but not out in real life.

Or maybe there are cages in real life too, but not made of wire like the dog cages stacked up at a puppy mill.

SHE had covered a lot of ground in HER 92 years. In fact, SHE talks to me – all the time about HER adventures. It makes my head spin.

I guess because SHE lives alone, I am the recipient of HER memory book. On and on SHE goes, about HER birth in New Haven Connecticut, being raised in New York City, with summers spent on a lake in Northern Maine.

SHE talks about HER days at Vassar in upstate New York, HER months working as an actress in Mexico City, with actors named Melvyn Douglas, Dame May Whitty, Gertrude Lawrence, Eddie Albert, John Forsyth, Charlton Heston…Never heard of any of them, but then I am younger than SHE, especially in dog years.

SHE describes HER three years in Paris where SHE fell in love with a married French doctor.

What a major mistake, in my opinion. (not in HER'S!) It seems so typical of a young American girl HER first time out and about in the world. A married doctor! And French!

I shake my head in disapproval. When I do so, my ears fly.

SHE was able to explore Spain, England, Germany, Switzerland,

Italy, Sicily, Greece, Tunisia, Algiers, Morocco, during those years in Europe. No wonder my head's in a whirl. SHE has really been around!

Then, I have to hear about a divorce in Charlotte Amalie, St. Thomas, the US Virgin Islands, and another divorce in Lake Tahoe, near Reno, Nevada.

With husband number two, SHE went to Israel five times in one year. SHE stayed in Tel Aviv, where HER husband looked out the window of the hotel and noticed on the beach next to it, some fat ladies spritzing themselves in the waters of the Mediterranean. "Just like Brooklyn," HER husband remarked.

Well, you can't take Brooklyn out of the man, or so they say – or maybe it's you can't take the man out of Brooklyn.

SHE is telling me how SHE went with him to a kibbutz in the hills near the Gaza Strip, one evening, as SHE is cooking our dinner here at home – a roast chicken with some boiled potatoes and carrots.

I can't wait for the tidbits.

"At that kibbutz, we had carrots and boiled potatoes but with no butter, no salt. No flavor at all – but even though the vegetables were so fresh from the enormous kibbutz farm, I don't know how they ate them. They were tasteless," SHE says, adding an extra dab of butter to our carrots.

SHE really isn't a snob, although that sounds like one…maybe just a snob about food and tasty things and especially treats.

SHE and that second husband, Louis, also stayed at the King David Hotel in Jerusalem. "There were bullet holes in the glass door of our bedroom facing the hills across the Dead Sea from where Palestinians had shot at the hotel."

Talk about dodging a bullet!

Then I have to hear about vacations in Montreal, Vancouver, Canada, Hawaii, Alaska.

It's not only Europe that SHE gets around… a world traveler. It's exhausting.

I still am curious about HER biting her nails. I notice SHE doesn't bite them now. HER hands are normal. What kind of cage could make

HER so anxious as to have such a habit? How old was SHE? What precipitated the act of biting?

With me, that's easy. I licked my paws because they hurt and to wipe away the blood. I still lick them when the old hurt recurs or a scab gets scraped, but with HER?

I am determined to find out. I do this by yapping. It is not only to get HER attention. It is to get HER to tell me more. After yapping until SHE grows annoyed, I begin to lick my paws frantically, trying to give HER the idea. Paws. Fingernails. Get it?

Finally, one day in October – I think it's October because the leaves on the trees are changing color (I told you, dogs see color!) it happened, and I was sorry because the memory made HER cry. Then I had to lick HER tears. They were salty, but SHE stopped crying.

"How much I love you, little dog," I heard HER say, oh so softly. That made me wag.

With a sigh, SHE tells me "I have another child, but we do not speak."

Did the little one die, I wonder. I wonder too about my many puppies. I know how when you lose them, a kind of agony descends that never goes away. SHE looks so sad.

I lick HER hands frantically, trying to stop their shaking.

"There's a cage of silence between us I can't penetrate," SHE whispers. "I've tried," and with that, SHE folds me in her arms like I am a puppy.

I knew it! I knew there was a cage…as SHE called it, a cage of silence, so different from my own, but a cage for sure.

Cages! They are not funny. I heard someone say once – I don't remember who it was or where it was or when it was - "always leave the cage door open so the bird can return."

Well, dogs are not birds. Leave our doors open and we'll skedaddle as fast as four legs can carry us. Who wants to live so confined, with wire and metal to cut the paws and only a set of bars to look through? Of course, me, with only one eye.

I am here now. I thank the God of Togetherness. I am here for HER – as SHE is here for me…my person, in HER arms, in my own forever home.

Chapter Four

NOW WE'RE TALKING

SHE knows about my eye, how it happened. My foster parent told HER that I was hit by a man with a large stick, when I was in the shelter. It was not at the puppy mill. We weren't allowed out of our cages there.

Later, after the puppy mill was closed down, and I was at the shelter, because we were allowed to play outside from time to time, the man with his stick would poke us to keep us in line, you know, that sort of thing.

One day, I guess I wasn't moving fast enough, and he swung the stick hard, and it hit me in the right eye with a great smack. It hurt so bad I howled. I howled all night. There was blood on my face and in my nose. A couple of days later, the eye was infected. I felt terrible, listless. Life wasn't worth living.

I couldn't see out of that eye ever again.

It wasn't until my foster parent came, thank goodness only a few days later that I had good fortune. The first thing she did was take me to a vet. He operated on my right eye, cleaned out the infection, and closed it. The vet also gave me medicinal baths for my fleas. It stung my backside because I had lost all my hair there and it was only raw, bare skin. Then he pulled out my rotten teeth.

Very quickly, I began to feel better. I would say I began to feel 'almost human' but of course that doesn't apply to dogs. Anyway, life had infinitely improved.

It was then SHE took me in. I could not believe it. A real house. A little bed of my own. HER big bed in which to spend the night in a small ball – right next to her warmth.

Now, in my forever home at last, I wouldn't trade one minute of one day for the life I lead!

I know SHE had dogs before me, but as SHE has said more than once, there is no substituting one for the other who has gone. "Each is unique. It's an entirely new relationship. The personalities are all so different."

I like that word 'unique' because what SHE and I have is like no other in the world. I know I am a bit possessive. Can't help it where SHE is concerned.

SHE told me of her first dog. SHE was only three years old and HER godmother brought HER a white spaniel puppy with liver-colored spots. HER father, a doctor, placed on the floor a dish of tomato juice for the puppy to drink. "Good vitamins," SHE remembers HER father saying.

SHE watched as the little dog put his two front paws into the dish as he drank. "Oh, Daddy," SHE remembers crying out. "His paws are red – they are bloody!"

Of course HER father reassured HER that it was only tomato juice. The dog was busy happily licking off his paws. "Thank goodness," SHE said, petting his small rear end. "I am going to call him Playboy."

There we are again. Paws. Fingernails. There's got to be a pattern. I am determined to figure it out.

While I do, SHE and I talk. We talk a lot.

When SHE is in her most voluble mood, SHE speaks of her three husbands. "The first – oh, lord I was so young – actually 22 years old, but naïve, so impressionable. He was 31, had been in OSS, stationed in London for four years during the blitz in World War 11. When he spoke to me of his time there, I felt like Desdemona, with Othello, the Moor, telling her tales of war. I was SO dramatic. Well, actress, at that time, was my profession."

I knew SHE was an actress. SHE told me all those names of people SHE had worked with. Sometimes, I think SHE still is! SHE can be so theatrical.

HER second husband was the one who took her to Israel. He was

Jewish, a PR man with his own firm in New York City. My how SHE runs on!

"Louis I never got over. We were married nine years – had two kids – plus two more, my step-children - a boy and a girl - from his previous marriage who we had only on weekends."

More kids! Sounds like a litter! And who is this Louis?

"Louis was larger than life, very charismatic."

It's funny. SHE seems to know my questions in advance.

"He was a split personality – Dr. Jekyll and Mr. Hyde – finally I realized he was making me sick. No really. I had to leave."

How sick? Did SHE have to throw up?

"He was really paranoid. He made me behave in ways where I didn't like myself. I wasn't me anymore."

Well you are you now! You' re SHE.

"Peter was my third. Are you listening little doggie? I want you to know all about me, because we're going to be together for a long time."

I give HER my snaggle-tooth smile, which always makes HER show HER teeth to me.

"Peter had such a great, embracing personality. We were married 23 years before he died at 75 of a heart attack. I miss him. He had such a sense of people – everyone was drawn to him. He had two sons from his first marriage, both of whom you will meet, Abbi. We are still close and their children are even closer to me."

Another litter?

"You will have great fun with them. They will love you."

I am lying in my bed on the couch. SHE is sipping HER vodka with Perrier and lots of ice. That's when SHE does most of the talking. SHE is too busy during the day.

"Did you know Peter had a wonderful yellow Lab, named Charlie?"

I shake my head as if in wonder.

"How he adored that dog. There is no question Peter was Charlie's person. The two would ride off in the Toyota in the mornings when we lived in Miami – 13 years in Miami, yet – Charlie in the seat next to Peter as he drove, 'riding shotgun,' as Peter used to say. I tell you, Abbi, they were a pair."

Like you and me I want to ask HER? But of course I can only make small, dog noises – not the usual yapping –but mini-snarls (not nasty), just to let HER know I'm listening. Are we a pair?

Somehow SHE gets the message and leans over to kiss the top of my head.

"You and me, Abbi," SHE whispers, scratching my ears. All I can do is wag my cropped tail, shut my one good eye and go blissfully to sleep, wondering how on earth SHE knows the answers to all my questions.

Chapter Five

BLIND DATES

"Each one of my husbands I met on a blind date," SHE says, sipping her tall drink. It is evening time. I can tell by the darkening sky we had just seen on our evening 'business' walk. It is after my supper – tonight the softened kibble with elegant bits of shrimp on top…a new taste experience.

Blind. I do not like that word. Blind date? What does that mean?

SHE explains. "A blind date is a meeting arranged by friends, between a boy and a girl who those friends think will be a match."

What does SHE mean by match?

"That the two – the boy and girl – man and woman – will like each other – maybe even become a couple."

What's a couple?

"Oh Abbi. I can tell by the look in that one good eye that you are puzzled." SHE shakes her head, takes a sip from HER tall glass. The ice tinkles as SHE sets it down on the coffee table in front of the red sofa.

"My first husband I met at a luncheon at The 21 Club in New york City. It was in October, and I had just turned 22 years old. This girl friend of mine thought I should meet this particular man, and she set up the blind date."

What is SHE rattling about? I still don't like that word 'blind'.

"Well, we hit it off. By the time I got home to my family's house uptown, there was a city telegram from him asking me to dinner. That was the beginning. We were married the following June."

Boy, that was fast!

"That was fast!" SHE repeats my thought. "His was a very wealthy family, his father a well-known art collector and a wonderful man. My father-in-law was a very private type – difficult to get to know – but for some reason, he grew fond of me… perhaps because his only daughter, also named Elizabeth – like me – had died of cancer at the age of 36, the year before I married his son. I kind of replaced her in his mind."

Or not! Like dogs…one can't replace the previous one. No way. Each is different, just like people. That's what SHE told me.

"Actually, my new husband and I had little in common. It wasn't long before I realized he looked at me as he would look at a stranger and the marriage was doomed."

I guess blind dates are really blind, and talk about a quick ending. I'm beginning to get the meaning. Blind…like an eye is blind…is the date blind? Or is it that you just can't see?

"At least I learned a lot about art," SHE says ruefully. "My father-in-law and I remained great friends even when I remarried seven years later – after my years in Paris."

Paris. Wasn't that the married Frenchman?

"Ah, Paris!" SHE lays her head back and looks at the ceiling. "I came alive there, restored my sense of self. I was able to explore – the world of art in Florence – the world of *cuisine* in France…well, you know that, Abbi. You tasted the cheese *soufflé* SHE says turning to pat my head. "I lived in Paris on the third floor of a house – right next to a house that belonged to Cole Porter - on the *rue Monsieur*."

Certainly an appropriate street name for YOU, *Madame*!

"It was very close to the Rodin Museum. What a glorious place, with its garden full of statues at the back of *L'Hôtel Biron*, the *château*-like building where Rodin lived and worked."

SHE takes a sip.

"From Paris, during my three years there, I was able to go skiing in Davos, Switzerland, stay in London with an actress friend from Mexico days and her family where they served a goose and plum pudding for Christmas dinner, swim at the Lido Beach near Venice, and dance the night away in Sitges on the Costa Brava in Spain."

SHE is making me dizzy!

"I was making myself dizzy!"

There we go again. Same wave length.

"Louis– husband number two – I also met through a girl friend. She had him come to her apartment just for a drink and to meet me. When he came into her front door, I saw that his dark brown eyes were the most intelligent I had ever seen."

What does that mean?

"Louis turned out to be the smartest person I ever met. That night, he took me to a jazz club in Greenwich Village. I have always loved jazz - - Miles Davis – Oscar Peterson - the big bands like Duke Ellington."

Enough with the music.

"We were married eight months later."

Another fast one! (and another sip for HER).

"The final blind date/husband material was really odd. I was separated from Louis – on the way to divorce. A young male friend – who was dating a great friend of mine – she was older than he – but so attractive – convinced me to double date…for me to join the two of them and a man named Peter."

Double date? Blind date? I must have had a quizzical look because SHE turns to me and says, "Abbi, a double date is when two couples go out for an evening together – to dinner or a concert or a movie."

I wag in response to let HER know I kind of understand.

"Well, it was all arranged, even though I felt it was much too early to be looking around again. After all, I was only separated."

Still married though? I shake my head, ears peaked.

"On the morning of the double date, my friend's young man had to go on business to St. Louis. 'We'll do it another time,' I remember saying. When I hung up, the phone rang and it was Peter, the blind date I was supposed to meet. 'Who needs them?' he questioned. 'Let's you and me meet at the Essex House on Central Park South – for a drink at least'."

"How will I know you, I asked?" 'I'll be wearing a Racquet Club tie,' Peter answered."

Huh? What's a dog know about 'a tie'? A leash? Or what's a Racquet Club?

"I had no idea what a Racquet Club tie looked like."

Hey. SHE and I are in the same boat!

"Peter said the tie was striped. Anyway," another sip, "I reluctantly agreed and went to the Essex House at the appointed time."

SHE really was going blind on this one!

"At the Essex House, there is a short hall before entering the bar, and as I walked it, I saw a man coming toward me. His tie was striped. I went up to him tentatively and said 'Peter?' He said with a big smile, 'No. The name's Bill, but I am more than ready to go and have a drink with you.' I said no, of course and stumbled my way into the bar."

SHE was stumbling?

"I wasn't really stumbling but I was nervous. I got there and saw a tall man at a table next to the bar-counter. He stood up and it was immediate…"

Why is SHE always in such a rush?

"He said, looking at me admiringly, 'For me?' with a wonderful smile. We sat down together. He ordered drinks for us both, as Bill came into the bar and stood next to our table, listening to every word we said… 'where'd you go to college?' and 'do you have brothers and sisters?' – you know, Abbi, things that strangers say to one another at first."

I have no idea what SHE's talking about. Dogs use the sniff test to get acquainted. Perhaps people do too… her perfume, his masculine musk?

"It was embarrassing, but then we had to laugh and Peter took me off to dinner and then dancing at the St. Regis Roof and within a year or two we were married. It lasted until he died 23 years later." SHE pauses. "I miss him," and tears fill HER eyes.

I lick HER hand in sympathy. SHE touches the top of my head and stops talking.

My lesson in blind dates is done.

Whew!

Chapter Six

A WALK IN THE PARK

One late fall day, SHE and I, on our walk about the park-like space around our community, met a man. Actually, his police dog made the first introduction, a strong, lively fellow who came up to me fast. He was at least 10 times bigger than I, but I set up such a yapping, jumping on all four feet (and I can jump pretty high), that it stopped him cold.

"Come here, Beau," the man said with a laugh, pulling on his leash. "That little dog is ready to eat you."

Little dog indeed! I have a strong, intimidating presence when I want to.

"Abbi, behave yourself," SHE said, drawing me close to HER sneakers.

"Well, they seem to know each other…my Beau, your Abbi," the man said with a smile. "I'm Steve – from across the street."

"And I'm Elizabeth," SHE said. I noticed the two of them were showing a lot of teeth – a friendly look to say the least. It wasn't like they were snarling or anything, and they kind of bowed to each other.

"Been here long?" Steve asked HER.

"It's been almost three years," SHE said.

"I've seen you before," he said. "Is that a new dog?"

"Well," SHE said, "yes. I've only had her a few weeks. Abbi's a rescue dog."

"They're the best," Steve responded. "They are so grateful."

Of all the pompous things to say! Right away, I did not like this

Steve. And I certainly did not like Beau, who was pushing toward me to do the sniff test, and I wanted no part of that, believe me! Grateful indeed! Of course I am thrilled to have a forever home and thrilled that SHE is my person. But who is this stranger who is flirting with HER and interrupting our walk.

"Can I join you in meandering?" he asked HER.

SHE nodded, much to my chagrin. "If we can keep the dogs apart."

The four of us walked on the street. This is a quiet community called The Harbor, although I have yet to see any water. There are over 200 houses and condos. It is for people over the age of 55. So, there are quite a few old folks – including HER. I have seen people with walkers walking and an old man with a cane, but there are other younger, more vigorous types as well.

Many of them have dogs! That is the best part of The Harbor. We as a species are much beloved and accepted here, treated like royalty and with respect. It sure is a change from my earlier life!

SHE and Steve are deep in conversation. My they can talk – but I already know that about HER. I keep my distance from Beau who gives me baleful looks from the other side of Steve. I can't wait for this to be over, and I can go home to my bed on the couch next to HER as SHE watches the evening news.

I sure hope this Steve thing isn't the beginning of a beautiful friendship. I can tell by the way he says goodbye to HER he wants more!

"If it's nice tomorrow, maybe we could do this again?" Steve had the audacity to say to HER. I was significantly alarmed when I saw HER kind of dimple and smile when SHE nodded assent. "That'd be nice," SHE said in HER softest voice.

Oh, I can tell by the timbre of HER speech what HER mood is. This moment was really alarming. Was Steve going to become a regular?

And that Beau? Will I have to put up with him too?

We finally get into the house and the red couch is there waiting and the apricot colored bed of mine is inviting me to leap into it and the news is on the television. SHE has her tall drink and is sitting beside me. SHE turns to me, pats my head and scratches under my chin (which I love because I can't do that by myself) and says, "That was kind of nice, now wasn't it, Abbi."

I look at HER with disgust.

"And Beau. What a handsome fellow. You were flirting with him, weren't you Abbi."

My head snaps up in astonishment. Flirting with that beast of a dog? SHE has got to be kidding. Any flirting that was going on was between HER and Steve, with all those tooth-filled grins at each other and HER simpering ways.

"I think I'll ask Steve to dinner, Abbi. What do you think? He can even bring Beau. Would you like that?"

With this remark, I leap out of my little bed and run into HER bedroom to hide.

"Hey come back Abbi," SHE calls after me.

In HER dreams!

"I need you to help me plan the menu. You think the cheese *soufflé*? Or is that too girlish. Maybe beef short ribs would be better. Steve seems like a manly man."

I am standing in the doorway of the living room just looking at HER. What is SHE thinking? A manly man? What's that? SHE's 92. Steve's got to be in his 80s – but I have to admit he's in pretty good shape. At least he doesn't need a cane or a walker.

I slowly creep back toward the red couch and my bed on the cushions beside HER. My head is down. I guess I have to accept the inevitable. SHE is not mine alone. I already knew that – from the family and grandchildren.

This Steve is a new threat, a different presence who will pull HER interest away from me, take up HER time which should belong to me, and perhaps – oh horror of horrors - even make HER love me less. I curl up in a little ball beside HER, feeling bereft.

SHE looks over at me. SHE senses my angst. SHE touches my head, oh so gently. "Don't worry …my little Abbi…you have nothing to worry about. You will always be first."

I told you. SHE always knows my thoughts. We are bonded, and I am able to fall asleep happily, chasing the rabbits in my dreams, paws twitching in my apricot bed.

Chapter Seven

THE DINNER PARTY

It was decided. Steve (and Beau – ugh!) were due for dinner! It was a Friday night, the first of November, a rather cold, blustery beginning of the new month. I felt it in my bones and it suited my mood. I was not looking forward to the evening.

And how SHE had prepared! I never saw such goings on – for the past week. First, SHE came home with the shopping…the perfect beef short ribs; onions, and mushrooms to enhance the beef, russet potatoes for the mashers with extra cream and butter, fresh Bibb lettuce, and virgin olive oil and "the perfect Merlot wine – two bottles one for the dining table, one for the pot!" SHE exclaimed happily. "And look at this Brie, Abbi. Perfectly ripe."

This all meant nothing to me, but as SHE prepared the ribs yesterday, I could hardly stand the delicious smell that came from the oven. Oh I was salivating! I even dreamed of the aroma all night long when I was sleeping next to HER.

"When I do it a day ahead, I can skim the fat off the top when it's cold and reheat it tomorrow, right before dinner. Also, the flavors will develop in the ice box over night," SHE explained.

I didn't care. All I knew was that my forever home smelled of heaven.

Then it happened. They came. Steve and Beau! There was something about both of them I did not trust.

SHE was wearing HER best dress – actually a silk top and pants – in black. SHE had on sparkly earrings I had never seen before and lots of lipstick. It made me nervous.

SHE had moved my bed off the red couch and put it on the floor! It was nearby, but I felt diminished and upset that THAT Steve was going to be next to HER in MY place! And that beastly dog, Beau? Where was he supposed to sit?

Steve had brought HER a bottle of red wine and a small bunch of pink roses. SHE placed the flowers in a vase, and I could tell by the way SHE eyed the wine, that it was *el cheapo*. SHE was not impressed.

Yay!

They were sitting there over what I guessed to be a martini with a garish olive in each stemmed glass. SHE had put out some mixed nuts, and the two just sat there talking. Beau, thank god, had gone to a corner of the room and was watching them – and me – from a distance. I lay on my bed – but fully awake and alert, mind you. I did not want to miss a trick.

I am a very observant dog. I notice things. I register how people behave. After all, I have to, to get along in life, to stay away from their feet, to avoid them when angry, and to assess their every mood – and thought.

I am studying Steve, as I lie here. He is glancing around the room, and I can tell he is in some way evaluating HER worth…if SHE could possibly be rich.

"What a wonderful painting," he says. "Where did you find it?"

"Oh, it was a gift from a father-in- law of mine, a long time ago. He bought it in Paris. He had quite a collection."

(Husband number One).

"A collection? Really."

"Oh, yes. He was one of the founders of The Museum of Modern Art. There are many of his pictures there – he has long since passed away – and there are pieces of his at the Metropolitan Museum as well."

Big mistake! I should start yapping to warn HER.

"In new York City, I presume?"

"Yes."

"Pretty impressive," Steve says, talking a long pull on his martini, extracting the olive and destroying it in small, self-satisfied bites.

I can't stand him. He's so obvious.

Finally, at the glass dining table, with both of us dogs underneath waiting for the crumbs to fall, they eat the beef ribs. I hear Steve say, "What a fabulous French feast! You are an amazing cook."

"Blame it on the *Cordon Bleu*," SHE answers, obviously pleased.

"You went there?"

I can just see Steve think, 'rich and a great cook'! But why can't SHE?

"Yes, I went there years ago, when I lived in Paris."

"You lived there?"

SHE's off again about her adventures – oh not the married French lover part – but enough to intrigue Steve – who talks about being a widower and how lonely he is and how he would love to go to France…

Hint, hint. Who's he kidding? And where's HER common sense? Nowhere in sight!

I have been listening and watching. I can see everything from under the glass table. I notice how he assesses the silver ware and the value of the other paintings, the quality of the linen napkins. He is surely on the make, and now I can tell, he sees a trip with HER to Paris!

At last the meal is over. As Steve rises – does he help clear the dishes? No! He goes to HER and takes HER hand. I decide it's time. I dart from under the table and start running in circles, doing my most strident yap.

"Abbi! What's got into you?" SHE cries out.

"What a little mutt," Steve says, annoyed.

This does it. I make for his trouser cuff and start yanking at it with the two fangs I have left in the front of my mouth. He kicks at me.

"Can't you manage your dog?" Steve asks HER, his tone nasty.

Beau has begun to bark, but thank goodness, he stands motionless. He's not getting into the fray.

"Come here, Abbi," SHE calls. I pay no attention, snarling as best I can with his cuff in my mouth and swinging around as he kicks his leg.

"Jesus!" Steve exclaims. "You should get rid of this…"

"What?" SHE is outraged. "Get rid of Abbi? You're crazy, mister.

She's my family!" And with that pronouncement, SHE leans down and grabs me in mid-air and hugs me to HER breast.

"Well, I guess the evening's over," Steve says in a subdued voice. He is shaking out his leg, inspecting the cuff. "The food was elegant. Thank you for that. I'll just get Beau now...and perhaps we can go walking again?"

I can tell Steve is reluctant to end things this way. He hates to leave the side of so obviously a well-to-do lady, and an excellent cook, who happens to live so conveniently near.

It's like he's waiting to be asked for a nightcap or something, but SHE is adamant. I can tell. To my delight, SHE says quietly, "We'll see. Goodnight Steve," and SHE moves to the front door.

I watch with bated breath. Steve kind of leans toward HER on the stoop, but SHE consciously moves back and away from him.

As soon as SHE comes back into the room, the first thing SHE does is pick up my bed and put it on the red couch where it belongs. It makes my heart full to see HER do this, to know that it is ME SHE wants next to HER, not that money-grubbing creep named Steve...and his measly dog, Beau.

I climb aboard my resting place. HER hand is scratching under my chin where I can't reach and prepare myself for a well-earned sleep. I have prevented disaster.

What a brave dog am I!

Chapter Eight

STALKER

Ever since arriving in my forever home a couple of months ago, SHE has always said, "Abbi, you structure me." I know what she means. SHE takes me out at dawn, just to the nearest tree, fussing at me because I am sleepy and it's hard to clip on the leash. "You can't go outside naked, Abbi," SHE exclaims with a laugh.

After my breakfast, around 7:30 in the morning, we go for a 'business walk'. It takes longer but I usually perform on cue. At noon, we leash up and go out again, as well as at 4:00 in the afternoon. My supper is around 5:30, after which there are treats (yum), a short digestive rest on my bed on the couch, and another 'business' meander. Finally, around 9:00, there is a nearest tree visit. That's it.

Since the short ribs of beef, French style dinner, our routine has changed somewhat. Because it is evident that SHE has decided to NOT go walking with Steve across the street (much to my approval – no avaricious Steve – no vicious Beau!) SHE is cautious, particularly at the noontime walk, and also the one at 4:00 o'clock.

SHE peeks out to see if his car is in front of his house. If it's not there – it's a green Ford- (I told you…dogs see color), we go out the front door as usual. If the vehicle is parked right in front, we go out of the back of our house through the garage and down a different street, praying he won't see us.

I call HER the artful dodger.

Steve's not dumb. Unfortunately, he figured it out and only yesterday, as we were walking down Brook Hills Drive, the street adjacent to Spring Meadows Lane, he pops up – with the massive Beau – and stands right in front of us.

"Ah, there you are," he says with a bright smile. SHE has turned quite white because he did startle both of us.

"So you've taken to walking a different route."

"Well, yes. We needed a little variety," SHE says.

Steve laughs. "Variety! I say, you don't find much of it around here at The Harbor."

"No, you don't," SHE says primly and we keep walking. We have increased the pace.

"You are moving quite swiftly, my dear…not in your usual leisurely fashion."

SHE gives a little laugh. "I'm trying to get a bit more exercise. It's important to keep moving, you know." At this point we are nearly running. I decide to yap in rhythm to our steps in hope that Steve and Beau will get the message - that we want to be alone.

They don't.

In fact, they are keeping up with us, making for quite an amusing looking picture – two people – two dogs, one yapping, one now barking - nearly running down Brook Hills Drive!

We finally gain the house. "Nice to see you, Steve," SHE calls gaily, and with a quick wave of HER hand, we find ourselves back in the garage in the dark as the door comes down dramatically, sealing Steve and Beau outside.

"Whew!" SHE says.

Hey. That's my word.

"We'll have to think of another route," SHE says, as we go in through the laundry room.

A different 'ruse', I think. I told you I had a good vocabulary, didn't I? Well, I do.

"It's too bad, really," SHE is mumbling as we walk into the living room. "He is quite a nice-looking fellow – and pleasant enough – and intelligent…"

And a moocher, I want to yell. Instead, I just start yapping. He's looking for someone with money to take him in…and I guarantee he'd go through every bit of yours if he could. Did you see how his eyes lit up when you mentioned the Museum of Modern art and The Metropolitan Museum and all those pricey pictures?

Of course I can't really say all these things – I wish I could. I can only stand in front of HER, looking up at HER, and chew HER out. SHE knows I'm angry with HER, that I am trying to tell HER something.

SHE looks down at me thoughtfully. "And you, little dog?" SHE regards me for what seems a long time, as I keep blathering. "I think I get it, Abbi."

Then. SHE goes over to the couch. I hop up into my bed. We sit together quietly for a long moment. We do not touch.

Finally, SHE turns to me. "I think, sweetheart, we have a stalker. I don't like it. I'm not sure what to do…how to avoid him. I don't think he's physically dangerous, do you?"

Hey. You never know I want to say, as I see HER go to prepare HER evening drink and prepare some sliced tomatoes for HER dinner. SHE comes back to the couch and turns on the television.

The news has a Breaking Story of a young woman murdered by a stalker in the city of Baltimore.

"Oh, she was so young," SHE says as SHE takes a hefty swallow of her drink.

Hey. I could use one myself!

Chapter Nine

A TAP AT THE DOOR

I fully expected it, knew it was coming. It happened three days after our running down Brook Hills Drive – away from those two.

They're back!

I see HER peek through the peephole in the front door.

"I know you're in there, …saw you go in with the dog," Steve almost shouts through the door. "You were carrying some books. Hey, what's up? Open up! It's been awhile." He is waving a (cheap) bottle of red wine. "It's getting to be that hour."

SHE slowly opens the door, stands squarely in the entrance.

"Sorry, Steve," SHE says resolutely. "I'm busy right now."

"You're not going to let me in?" He shakes the bottle in front of her. The gesture is almost threatening. Beau is standing close to his master. He is emitting a low growl.

"Not now, Steve."

"Later?" He asks.

What an insolent fellow!

"In future, why don't you give me a call before you come over. I'm sure you have my number. It's in The Harbor's registry."

"Boy. You're suddenly so formal."

"No. It's just not convenient now," and SHE proceeds to close the door.

He puts his foot in the doorway, stopping the process.

I let out a major yap. This is unacceptable.

"That dog of yours really hates me," Steve says.

"Somehow you frighten her. And by the way, her name is Abbi," SHE says haughtily.

Frighten me? Hah. SHE's got to be kidding.

"Just a sec. You mad at me?" Steve has his hand up now, leaning against the doorjamb.

"No. Why would I be?"

"I can't guess...but your attitude...well, it's different." Beau is standing at attention.

I decide to make my presence felt by standing next to HER, making myself as tall as possible. I am only nine pounds (maybe a bit more, what with all the treats) and probably as many inches high, but I feel formidable as I stare at Beau.

"Please Steve. I don't mean to be rude, but I'm busy."

Steve remains in place, his shoe in the doorway. He seems really confident, laid back.

That does it for me. How smug can you get? I aim at his foot in the doorway, yapping as loud as I can, which of course, sets Beau off to a nasty snarling, and to prevent a dog fight, Steve finally retreats. SHE closes the door.

SHE looks down at me. "Thanks, Abbi. But you've got to be careful. Beau's a lot bigger than you."

And Steve! He's a lot bigger than YOU.

SHE gives me a startled look when I think this, as if SHE knows exactly what I'm thinking.

When I look back, the only real dogfight I ever got into, I lost. It was in the beginning, at the puppy mill. I had just gone into heat for the first time when, I was set upon by more than one dog. I was bloodied. I kind of gave up. What else could I do?

After that, I became very docile, very shy... and the puppies. They kept coming until – well, you know the rest.

I wonder about HER...HER first. Did SHE have to fight? Did SHE learn how? Do I have to fight for HER now? Doesn't SHE get what Steve's all about? I know SHE and he are old, but hey, you never know, and for him, it's the money for sure and maybe a forever home with HER.

Over my dead body! This is MY forever home, not his. Not Beau's! No way, *José.*

Now, I'm spayed. I have no fleas. My teeth – what's left of them – are clean. I am strong, and I'm a fighter.

Beau better watch out. He better not fool with me. I can psych him out, even though he's much bigger than I. I can run rings around his long legs, nip at his heels, and yap at him at a high decibel. Back off, Bub, and that goes for your master, Steve, too.

As I am thinking these things, SHE leans down and ruffles the hair on my head and behind my ears, and says, "I wish I had your fight, little dog. For one so small, you are the brave one. You are my Abbi."

I can only look up with love and smile, showing what teeth I have left.

I told you. We communicate.

Chapter Ten

CRY BABY

It is that time of day, after the Steve/Beau intrusion. We are sitting – me in my bed – on the red couch. SHE has her tall glass and there is lasagna in the oven. I can smell it. Even though I have had my supper – and it was good – it always is – I anticipate HER having HER's.

Later, I know SHE will take tiny bits of the noodle part, cool it, and give it to me as SHE dines. It's happened before, and though SHE calls me "beggar dog" – because I do make little whines at HER feet, I can only tell HER, "Who's fault is that?" After all, SHE started it.

Now, as we sit on the couch, SHE tells me a story. "You know, Abbi, at one time I was chairman of a shelter for dogs and cats. It was called Bide-A-Wee Home, and we had a big property out in Westhampton. Long Island, and one in Wantagh, and a building in New York City."

A whole building in the city? In Long Island, could the dogs run around on grass?

"In Westhampton, we had dog runs with doors that led directly out into a fenced yard. It was large and had trees and the dogs could play together all day and meet potential adopters out there."

Boy. Not my shelter. Lucky fellows at Bide-A-Wee.

"Every year, we would have a big gala in New York – usually at The Plaza or The Pierre Hotel. Hundreds of people would come. They were animal lovers who donated to Bide-A-Wee, because you know, Abbi, it's expensive to run an animal shelter."

I'll bet. All that food! The vets. The caretakers.

"After 9/11, when the city was hit – the Twin Towers – there were cadaver dogs down at the site."

Ugh.

"We had our vets down there too, taking care of those wonderful animals, who would lie upon the hot rocky, shattered debris when they knew a body was caught beneath. Talk about brave."

I couldn't do it!

"Their paws and stomachs would be burned and even psychologically, those dogs knew exactly what they were doing and how hard it was."

SHE takes a sip of HER drink. The aroma from the oven almost makes me drool. SHE continues.

"I have to tell you one funny story, Abbi. Always, at our galas, we had animals. One year, we were honoring the NYCPD police dogs and their handlers. There was one beautiful, big, handsome police dog, named Renfrew."

Like Beau? That big? I don't like him already.

"Well, Renfrew had caught a thug raping a young woman out in the wooded area at LaGuardia airport. He and his police person caught the man in the act and Renfrew even bit the man right in the buttocks."

"Ouch!"

"Anyway, at the gala, Renfrew and his policeman came up on the small stage and as this handsome, lion-like creature turned around and saw the audience of so many people staring at him, he kind of slumped down and started to whimper." SHE laughs. "That gorgeous scary animal was crying!"

If dogs could laugh, I would. The picture of the large beast, sitting there, whining, was too much. And I thought he was supposed to be a fighter!

As always, SHE picks up on my thought. "It's almost laughable," SHE says. "There he was – Renfrew, the great – able to – on command, of course – turn into a lethal animal – but in real life, just a softhearted creature like the rest of us. Renfrew's policeman, with whom the dog lived, adored him and said he was the most loveable of animals."

That's hard to believe. I know I'm skeptical, but I know DOGS.

"In any case, Renfrew was the hit of the gala and Bide-A-Wee made a lot of money that night, partly because of him." SHE kisses me on the top of the head. "You're my fighter! But you have to behave yourself."

Now, what does SHE mean by that?

"You can't go yapping at Beau anymore. He could swoop you up in one bite."

Ouch again. Wouldn't want him to take a piece out of my backside… what there is of it.

"So please. We'll keep Beau and that Steve at arm's length. But Abbi, you have to cool it," SHE says, leaning down and almost whispering in my ear.

Doesn't SHE realize I am quicker, more agile, than Beau, that even though he has the muscle and the poundage, I can be like an annoying little flea and drive him crazy. I know all about fleas, believe me. I learned the hard way.

Then SHE leans down once more and I hear HER say, "And now, Abbi. Lasagna?"

Oh yes, oh yes… my favorite time of day… sharing HER dinner, or as they say, breaking bread together.

Chapter Eleven

DISCIPLINE!

Boy, do I chew HER out!

I yap in circles, my tone angry, in order for HER to learn to mind HER manners. 'Course, I'm only kidding, but I want HER to know SHE left me ALONE in the house for several hours and that's unacceptable.

How dare SHE?

I miss her, every time.

When SHE goes out, SHE always returns with packages and bags from the grocery store – with treats for me inside! (That's good.) Or SHE will appear with HER hair clean and shining and all bloused up. This happens once a week. I have to get used to it.

While SHE is away, I usually sleep a bit, then hop up on the back of a red chair and look out the window waiting impatiently for HER return. Sometimes, I see a guy, one of the landscapers in our complex, clipping the hedge right next to the side of the house. (Sometimes SHE will tell me my jagged hair is like a neglected hedge. SHE's only kidding, of course.)

If I let out a series of yips, I see the guy jump! (Ha, ha.) He looks so startled. It's funny.

When SHE is home here with me, it is my dream come true. Any dog would feel the same – perhaps even a cat too, but that I sure wouldn't know.

SHE told me SHE wrote something on the computer about me, can you imagine? I feel flattered that SHE would do that.

"What's it all about, Abbi?" SHE coos to me. "I've written a little love letter to you. Do you want to hear it?"

And SHE reads it to me.

"To Abbi: I've had many dogs. Each has given me an experience of life and love in different terms. Each was precious. But at the end of the journey – which is approaching for you and for me, because, you know, as a wise man once said, we are only here on this earth for a visit – you, my Abbi, are sweetest of all. We can brave whatever comes, and face our Forever and Ever Home hand in paw, for surely, we will be together there."

Although I don't really understand all the words SHE utters, I can tell by the tone of HER voice exactly what SHE is saying and I want to lie down and die of love.

After hearing all this, I guess I better stop scolding HER so much. I do it a lot and perhaps it isn't fair.

But I have got to teach HER discipline, now don't I?

SHE told me once about HER father. He was a tough man in many ways, although SHE loved and respected him a lot. In the summers up in Maine, on the lake where HER family had a log cabin, in the very early morning, HER father would have HER row a boat on the lake so he could catch fish for breakfast.

There were lake trout and bass and perch in the fresh water that were exceptionally delicious fried in cornmeal in a black skillet – right out of the lake, ready to jump in the mouth! When SHE describes this to me, I start to drool. Sounds SO good!

When SHE was rowing, HER father would not let HER say a word. 'Don't want to frighten away the fish,' he would declare. SHE found this unreal, because the sound of the oarlocks was louder than anything SHE might say. SHE knew he did not want to be bothered with HER thoughts.

It made HER sad because, as a young girl, it was a moment when SHE might have bonded with HER parent in the privacy of a boat on a lake.

"Maybe that's why I talk so much, Abbi," SHE says to me. "My father had a way of shutting me down."

Now this makes ME sad. I don't mean to be so tough on HER. SHE's not spoiled, I realize, at least, not always. SHE had told me of HER hard work at college – SHE went during the World War II years and it was difficult because in 1943, America was losing the war in the

Pacific. SHE went through the usual four-year college experience in two and a half years.

"It was hard," SHE told me. "But the war was on and we were all determined to get out of school and go fight for our country. Of course, when I graduated in 1946, the war was over. The atomic bomb had fallen on Hiroshima, Truman was in office and Franklin Delano Roosevelt, dead in April, 1945."

I can see SHE looks wistful. It must have been tough…must have taken a lot of discipline to get through a demanding college curriculum so fast. Beats me how SHE did it but SHE did.

"You know, Abbi, one of the most moving moments of my life was when Roosevelt died. The war was still in full force – in Europe and in the Pacific. There was still a year for it to go. When our President died, we didn't know what or how things would happen, if we would succeed."

Whew! (My favorite word). It must have been scary.

"Vassar College is in upper New York State next to the Hudson River. Hyde Park, Roosevelt's estate was north of us. The railroad traveled next to the river. I remember standing on a hill overlooking the tracks with a candle in my hand and watching the train slowly moving toward his home at Hyde Park where our President would be laid to rest."

His Forever and Ever home, I think.

"We all stood there sobbing. The car in which his body lay had a huge American flag draped over it. It was so moving. We were all undone."

I know. I know. A bunch of girls. Don't mean to be uncaring. It must have been a rare and emotional event, but you know us females. We can be a bit over-emotional. Even me.

"Enough of that," SHE says matter-of-factly. "Enough of memory lane! Now what's for your supper?"

Oh, yay. Yay. Best time of day.

"How about your warm kibble with a topping of leftover lamb chop. No bones, of course. Just the sweet meat."

I think I'll give up disciplining HER anymore. How can I when SHE is SO good to me, and I trot off to the laundry room and wait by my bowl, hopping with anticipation as SHE comes to retrieve it and fix my DINNER.

Chapter Twelve

RAIN

I really hate rain. And wind! When it blows hard, I feel like it's going to pick me up and send me sailing.

I told you. I'm small. Once 9 pounds, but now, with all the good eating, I'm probably near 11, but still small enough to fly away if the wind is strong.

On the television, they say a big storm is coming – with thunder and lightening. I guess I'm not very brave. I cower at the loud claps and hide my head under the pillow in my bed. Yes, it has its own pillow made in the shape of a bone.

I think it's partly because I only have the one good eye that I frighten easily. Sometimes, I only see shapes, and if they are big and dark and tall – like the man with the stick who took my eye – I cringe.

"It's okay, Abbi," SHE will say. "I'm right here. Nothing to be afraid of," and SHE will usually give me a treat, just a little one.

I don't mind getting a little bit wet, but if it's really pouring, I'm miserable. Of course, sometimes it is absolutely necessary for me to go out – you know – 'business' – even as heavy drops come down. Afterwards, SHE always dries me off with a kitchen towel (which SHE then throws into the washing machine).

This Saturday, HER grandson, who will be home from college for the weekend, is coming over to give me a shampoo. SHE has the concoction all ready – it has oats in it which apparently is good for the skin – and Stanton – that's his name – will wash me in the bathtub.

I wonder if I'll end up with hair as bloused up as HER'S, after a beauty parlor visit. What a pair we'll be!

And it happens. Stan arrives midday on Saturday. He decides to use the kitchen sink as tub because it has a spray attachment. I'm there with the warm water in my curly hair, which feels quite grand, and he froths me up and rinses me off good.

"Abbi looks like a plucked chicken," SHE says with a laugh.

Huh? A plucked chicken? What does SHE think SHE looks like, standing in the shower, naked as a jaybird?

"Those tiny bones," SHE is telling Stan. "Be sure you get her whiskers. That little beard picks up bits of her supper, even twigs from the yard."

I feel like a baby in the sink. It really is delicious.

"Have you ever seen such a bedraggled dog?" SHE says with delight, as Stan takes me up in his big hands and wraps me in a fluffy white towel.

Then it's rubdown time. It tickles me and feels so good against my usually scratchy skin – that white towel. This goes on for a long time, it seems, and then Stan looses me on the floor where I do a dandy caper or two. I smell of honey (there's some in the shampoo, I was told), and what a great way to smell!

Hey. I feel like an entirely new dog, and SHE is palavering over me and telling me how cute I am and what a good girl I was and oh, how sweet it is to be under HER lavish loving. So I do another caper or two to let HER know how grateful I am to belong to HER.

Oh yes, how sweet it is!

Chapter Thirteen

PEANUT

That's his name, the Chihuahua next door. He and his owner just moved in. Oh, Steve, and that dog, Beau, are still around. We always try to avoid those two, but Peanut, now he's a different case entirely. He's cute.

I don't even mind him giving me nasal inventory. And I return it in kind.

"Abbi," SHE says, "I think you have a new boyfriend."

I shake my head so vigorously, my ears fly, but secretly...well, who knows? Maybe SHE's right.

It's a nice older gentleman next door, well, not older than SHE (no one is!), but certainly not young. I like the way he treats Peanut. For one so small – as small as me – it is nice to be treated with the respect we deserve.

When SHE and I go walking – SHE is using a cane now outside (not at home) – we often run into Peanut and his owner. We always stop to parlay a bit. It's been getting cold – winter approaching. SHE has bought me a fine, new coat to wear with Velcro straps. It's pale blue with dark blue trim, fits tight around my middle and has a little navy blue skirt with a pink bow. I wear it proudly. It's girly and pretty so I feel *femme fatale-like* in the outfit.

"My. Isn't Abbi *The fashionista!*" Peanut's owner declares, as I primp and preen before him (and Peanut).

"Yes!" SHE exclaims. "Very *chic*, don't you think?"

Here we go with the French words. Hey, SHE didn't buy this outfit in Paris, for heaven's sake.

The following Sunday, we are out and about for my final 'business' walk. It's about 6:30 and it's getting dark. I am in my coat and doing what I'm supposed to do when Peanut and his owner approach us. I notice Peanut's right foot is limping. He's got a white bandage around it.

"What happened to Peanut?" SHE asks, concern in HER voice.

"Poor little fellow. He twisted his leg…got it caught in a grating in the street, there over by the crosswalk. I had the devil of a time extricating that foot…'course, took him to the vet. He has a bad pulled tendon, don't you Peanut," he said, leaning down to pat the dog. Peanut has a coat on too – a dark green sweater with sleeves.

Sweaters are hard to get the legs in. I know. Like it's hard for HER to get HER socks on. Everything – all the little things – get harder as one gets old.

Tell me!

Peanut limps over to me, gives a little lick to my ear. I feel for his pain. We dogs are philosophical about hurts. We have patience. We give up to pain…just part of the journey…even when it really hurts…hey, we have major nerve endings too…but we're no crybabies.

I give Peanut a lick on his nose.

SHE's pretty good about pain, but SHE makes it clear when SHE hurts! I know right away when SHE's hit at night with miserable leg cramps or when SHE has been to the eye doctor and gotten a shot in HER bad left eye.

SHE really lets you know it's painful with HER 'Oohing and Aahing' – not what we dogs do. We bear these things in silence, resigned to fate.

We know it's no good to make a fuss. For what? It doesn't make the hurt go away, now does it!

Oh, I have restless nights, haunted dreams of puppies gone. I get sad, but I'm too proud to show it.

Like Peanut. I can tell he's a proud dog. He even smiles, although I can tell his leg bothers him.

"You're a little *femme fatale* with Peanut, Abbi," SHE says.

Again with the French words. And what does being a *femme fatale* even mean? I sure don't know.

"You're a flirt," SHE says as if in answer to my questioning thoughts. "And Peanut appreciates it."

I have no idea about that, but it pleases me SHE thinks so.

"You're a little cougar, Abbi," SHE says laughing. "He's much younger than you."

Cougar? Hey I'm a dog.

I do enjoy walking beside Peanut, sniffing the grass and twigs where he has sniffed, checking out a tree limb together. I think he likes me because he does give me a look and a lick from time to time. (It doesn't mean much. We've both been fixed – but I'm so happy he finds me appealing.)

If that's what being a *femme fatale* is, I'm all for it. Guess I'll keep doing my thing. I have to play a bit mysterious. That's important to a *femme fatale*. At the same time, I let him walk ahead of me, let him have the first crack at the roadside hydrant, let him play master of the Universe, because I, Abbi, know in my heart, Peanut loves me.

Hey. Miracles do happen.

Chapter Fourteen

NEW LAW IN CALIFORNIA

"Hey, Abbi, get this," SHE says to me this morning as I am eating my morning warm kibble. SHE seems excited, but I keep on munching. Nothing disturbs me while I eat.

"It's right here in the paper. 'All dogs, cats and rabbits from shelters sold in pet stores…'"

Rabbits? I never saw a rabbit at that awful shelter where I lost my eye. Sometimes I chase rabbits in my dreams. SHE says my legs are sometimes running in my sleep.

"'…in the state of California must now come directly from shelters and nonprofit rescues, instead of breeders or notoriously cruel puppy mills.'"

Puppy mills? I stop chewing.

"'Many puppy mill dogs provided to (and bought by) pet stores to sell, turn out to be sick, short-lived, with congenital psychotic behavior,'" SHE reads on.

I believe it. Having so many pregnancies and births leaves the mom-dog worn out and allows for bad genetics. I always worried about that with my pups.

I was used, as were the other females, all of us, breeding machines. The thought ruins my breakfast (what's left of it – only a few scraps).

"I guess, from what they write here, that nothing in the new law that stops people from purchasing an animal from a private breeder. Well, I guess that's only fair…if your some snobbish sort."

Yeah! Has to be pure bred! What a crock.

"Wow!" SHE exclaims. "'Anyone who violates the new law will face penalties as high as $500 per pet.' Now, that's terrific. They say that other states may try to enact the same law."

A big win for us four-legged females, I'd say!

"And hey, Listen to this, Abbi," SHE goes on, again reading from the paper. "Here's a story about a Labrador dog named Lulu. 'Lulu flunked out of bomb school, C.I.A. says.' She was being trained to detect explosives in cars and luggage. 'Clearly, Lulu was not enjoying herself,' the article goes on. 'Lulu soon had a new home. She was adopted by her handler and now spends her unemployment sniffing out rabbits and hanging out with a dog named Harry.'"

Oh, happy ending. Good for Lulu. She's my kind of dog. Who wants to spend their time detecting nasty smelling weapons of destruction? Not me! And, Lulu's got her friend Harry! I know how she feels.

After all, I've got my friend Peanut.

That stuff about the new law in California is really something. It's about time that at least some people recognize the cruelty – the brutal treatment – we female, puppy-producing machines are subjected to.

Maybe other parts of the country will create similar laws. Let's hope so.

These days, with all the sexual harassment cases going on – where men in power assault young women - hey, aren't puppy mills the biggest harassment of all? Us girls forced to produce litters by unknown male dogs? Sometimes it was so violent – ugh. I don't want to think about it anymore.

Anyway, thanks California. Hope you've started a trend!

Chapter Fifteen

MINI ME

Sometimes SHE calls me that.

"My little Mini Me," SHE will say. I guess it's because SHE identifies with me, that in someway, somehow, I am a tiny version of HER. Our two different species have so much in common, although we dogs have sensibilities so highly developed, that a person just can't understand them or compete with them. Like our sense of smell! It's awesome!

Also, we dogs have an extraordinary reaction to change of mood, change of voice tone, a change in the happiness/sadness quotient in humans.

For instance, I can tell intuitively when SHE is angry at her computer (often!) Then, I avoid HER at all costs.

Or I notice that SHE is being forgetful about turning off the stove. I bark to remind HER. Sometimes, SHE is furious at politics on TV, and I let HER curse away until the anger is gone. I leave HER alone and bury my head under my pillow.

I am HER alter ego in so many ways. That's how close we are.

I guess SHE also refers to me as Mini Me because sometimes I try to make it so you can't see me at all. I can be really MINI. It's a way of escaping. I make myself so small in my head for a bit until I get scared that I might fall into a ditch full of oil or a hole with lawnmower clippings. When the leaf blowers come, I quiver. They could take me up with the mulch and blow me away.

When this happens, I shake myself – ears flying – and emerge from my smallness as the brave, loud-mouthed, formidable dog that I really am.

SHE knows when I disappear like that and lets me alone, respecting my need to escape inside my body and pretend I don't exist. It's the only way I know to obliterate the pains of the past. Oh, I don't dwell on them. Never! But sometimes, in my dreamscape, the hurts recur and I cry in the night.

SHE hears me. SHE touches me, and only then can I return to restful sleep.

So, I am glad to be HER Mini Me, because SHE does the same thing, disappearing inside for a little while. When SHE comes back to real life, SHE will tell me stories of HER past. "My last and best husband, Peter, loved to gamble. When he'd lose at the track – and I mean a lot of money – he would grow depressed and unreachable."

I'm trying to understand.

"When I was divorcing husband number 2 – Louis – Peter came to visit me in Lake Tahoe where I was waiting my turn at the divorce court in Reno."

He visited while SHE was in the middle of getting a divorce? Is that legal?

"We went to a casino one evening - I think it was called The Palace Casino – just to, you know, have a night out and about, and I remember being shocked – no horrified – at seeing, in the parking lot, a huge, round concrete slab that was covered with bodies."

People bodies?

"Real people bodies. In the semi-dark, I could see legs and arms and heads, all still – as if they were the limbs of the dead."

Wow! (Another of my favorite words).

"I exclaimed to Peter, what are all those people doing, lying out here in the parking lot?"

"They're not people," he said. "They're children."

"Children, I questioned?"

"Yes. Their parents are inside, gambling the night away."

"Peter absolutely understood. I didn't. The fact that those little kids of all ages lay out there, often all night long, didn't bother him in the least, but it did bother me."

So all those little mini-me children lay out in the night while their mommies and daddies played games until the dawn broke over Lake Tahoe.

Whew. I agree with HER. I don't understand either. All I know is it wouldn't happen with my pups. No way

Chapter Sixteen

A BRAVER DOG I NEVER KNEW

That's what SHE says about me. I hear HER tell it to strangers, to Peanut's person, even to Beau's owner, Steve. Don't know if it's true, but it sure makes me prance with happiness.

Brave? I don't know, because I yap at HER? SHE knows it's only for attention. Perhaps it's because I scared Steve and Beau away. I'm more like Lulu the Labrador who was kicked out of the C.I.A. because she didn't like the job of sniffing for explosives. Can't say I blame Lulu. Now that dog is busy running after rabbits and field mice. Lucky Lulu.

SHE has taken to a new trick. SHE barks back at me. It makes no sense. I know SHE does it to shut me up.

It works.

I stop.

Although SHE doesn't know the language or what SHE's saying with her yaps, SHE gets her point across.

It's pretty hilarious.

SHE will even pretend to growl, calling me "growly bear" when I 'grr' to get attention (crumbs at HER dinner).

"It's my old age talking, Abbi," SHE tells me with a laugh.

Pretty laughable indeed because HER barks just add up to sound, although they do give me pause. (no pun intended). My yips and growls mean something. HER'S are just noise in my ears, mere babbling.

I am the communicator. SHE tells me I have a 'Napoleon complex', that I act all powerful and strong because I am so little. This makes no sense to me so, when SHE calls me that, I just puff up and swagger round to show HER who's boss.

Sometimes when I am my yappiest, SHE will laugh at me and tell me, "Abbi, you are SO scary." I know SHE is kidding, and I don't mind HER funning me. It's just HER way, and I cuddle up and all is forgiven.

I must say I am pretty brave when SHE washes my whiskers. They are quite long and fuzzy so they pick up bits of my supper and twigs when we're out walking. The latter has become a problem because I always keep my nose firmly on the ground. There is so much to inspect - so many messages from previous walking dogs and small nests of bugs and worms to explore. I come home with a forest of greenery on my face and of course, out comes the washcloth!

SHE never uses soap. Doesn't want to get it in my mouth or eye. No, it's just warm water but sometimes SHE has to scrub quite hard.

That's when I'm brave. I just submit and don't make a sound.

As I said earlier, I think a brave act on my part was getting rid of Steve and that big dog, Beau. I saved HER from HERSELF. Steve was no good. He had his eye on the prize – SHE and her money. I knew it instinctively. SHE did not.

I don't know if SHE realizes now how I saved HER, but I do, and it makes me proud.

Chapter Seventeen

QUEEN FOR A DAY

"I was in London during the coronation of Queen Elizabeth, back in June of 1953. Did you know that, Abbi?"

Now how would I know that! That's silly.

"The Queen loves Corgi dogs. She has several of them and they live in a palace and are treated like royalty."

The lucky beggars probably eat roast beef every day!

"Did you know the Queen and I are the same age?"

Again! How would I know that!

"In 1952 – she was so young – to be Queen of all England and I remember, when the crown – which weighed a ton – was set upon her head by the Archbishop – in the Cathedral – I saw her slender neck sag and almost buckle. It was so poignant. She bore the weight of the world"

Wow. Poor little Queen.

"I felt it such an honor to be there. It was a major moment, and I was witness," SHE says with satisfaction. Then, " Abbi you're my little Queen."

Hey! Queen for the day.

"You bear the weight of the dog world on those shoulders with bones like chicken wings…"

A Queen…with chicken wings?

"No one should have to live in a puppy mill with steel and wire cages and be used over and over again, " SHE continues. "But you survived. And the important thing, in spite of all your pain and troubles, - the blinding of your eye, your war with fleas that left your backside raw, your hurting teeth - somehow you maintained that sweet disposition. I cannot imagine you ever being mean and I love you for that."

I can tell SHE is saying something nice by the look in HER good eye. That's how we communicate. I know I don't really carry the weight of the world of dogs on my shoulders – nor do I wear a crown on my head – but I am totally aware of HER appreciation of my wayward life.

Before I came to my forever home with HER, I was a listless dog. I hadn't much spirit. I just let life take me where it would. But my world changed. I am treated like a Queen – from my new sporty coat and the delectable foods to eat and the softness of my small bed and HER large one.

Well, all I can say is that no palace in the town of London can compare. And now, when SHE and I go out for a stroll, I walk like I'm leading a parade to show the world of other dogs that live in The Harbor that I have a person of my very own.

Queen Elizabeth, move over. I've got you beat! Who needs a palace and a pack of Corgi dogs?

It's funny. That's HER name – Elizabeth, and SHE is my Queen for real. So SHE was in London for a majestic event but that's hardly all; SHE traveled on the famous Orient Express from Paris to Venice; bussed the length of Italy; plied the transatlantic steamers from New York to Europe; yachted in the Caribbean!

Why, I've never even been as far as downtown, and I certainly haven't ever rocked around in a train or boat or plane. But that's HER. That's my Queen, Queen of travel, for sure.

Now what's for dinner? I can smell a split pea soup SHE is cooking with a ham bone in its broth. I hope SHE will save me a bit of the leftover ham – a honey-baked ham, yet! Knowing HER, I am sure I'll find some minced up on top of my kibble. SHE always adds something extra tasty.

How could I possibly want to be anywhere else in the world than here in my forever home? Not in London. Not in Paris. Not on the high seas. I'll happily stay right here, next to the Queen in my life and the bubbling, delicious smelling pot on the stove.

Who could ask for anything more?

Chapter Eighteen

A MURMURING HEART

I am told I have a heart murmur. Don't know what that means. It doesn't murmur to me. I can't hear it.

"It's just something to watch," SHE tells me. "We've got a good vet."

I don't want to think I'm fragile. I look at HER beseechingly.

"Sweet Abbi," SHE says. "You know, with that little face, you make me feel purer."

Now what does SHE mean? Purer than what?

SHE gets my question. Must be in my stare from the good eye, because SHE adds, "It's just that there is something so innocent about you – so authentic – that…well, let's just say, you make me feel better than I really am."

Huh? I don't quite understand. Perhaps as time passes, I will.

Time. I don't know how to count it. I'm just a dog. It just happens – like a river you're paddling in that moves you along. Somehow each moment is all one with the other moments that tick, tick, tick you forward.

Anyway, I'm getting tired. My heart murmur is beginning to speak to me – for the first time. Little twitches. Each one stops me in my tracks.

SHE always notices and waits beside me until I start to move. After it happened several times, late last winter – I know because the air was really cold – SHE took me to the vet.

He was a nice man with gentle hands. When he spoke to HER in a low voice, I saw tears in HER eyes.

Okay. I get it. Trouble ahead

Even though my heart may murmur, it now belongs to HER. A piece of it also belongs to Peanut. Totally different feelings of love, but what a wonderful world to live in! Love in all the places that count. Even we dogs want to be loved. All SHE ever wanted – always – was to be loved. And SHE is. Boy is SHE!

By me. The beauty is it's mutual.

Why did SHE travel so much? Why was SHE running? From what? Or from whom? T'is a mystery.

SHE dreams at night like I do – but not of lost pups. SHE dreams of HER ancestors in Conestoga wagons crossing the Great Plains. SHE dreams of France and its checkerboard squares of green fields and great *allées* of trees. SHE dreams of the winds of Scotland from which her mother's family came, and she dreams of her father's Dutch heritage.

SHE has no need to tell me this. I can feel it as I lie next to HER at night, caught under HER arm. Those dreams are transmitted, one by one, but the mystery of HER life is yet unsolved.

Funny. It doesn't seem to matter – not matter at all – because it's me and SHE against the world.

And there's also Peanut.

They say a dog stops eating when he/she is in trouble…loses the appetite. Well, no problem tonight! Not yet, anyway even though lately, I find I'm eating less.

I still have my taste buds! I can't wait for my supper. I hope it's the stuff they call 'Top Sirloin Flavor', my favorite.

Chapter Nineteen

MY FOREVER AND EVER HOME

A lot of time has passed, at least in dog terms…several months for sure. The summer is over. It is autumn. I get easily startled. Yesterday, while out on our 'business walk', a bird suddenly seemed to fly straight at me. Of course, it wasn't really aiming at me, but I jumped, and my heart went racing.

It is now October again and leaves will do it too, make me jump – the big, fat, dry autumn leaves. They rustle and when the wind suddenly picks them up and hurls them at me, I am scared.

You have to remember I am not very big. It would be easy to crush me by mistake.

Lately, I find I get very tired. I think SHE gets tired easily too because the two of us seem to sleep a lot. It's amazing how alike the two of us are. I can smell the tiniest scent and learn from it. SHE can read a book and come to know great things. I can sleep in the hollow of HER arm. SHE rests against me as if we are one.

When I am sad – for my lost pups, for those still in the puppy mills - SHE senses it and pets me gently, ruffling my curly hair. When SHE is sad, I see HER cry – for HER lost child or a friend who has died - and I go and carefully lick HER cheek, where the salty tears lie.

I had a tremor today. Oh, I have had them before. It takes my whole body and it trembles me. For seconds, I don't know where I am. Today's was the worst.

When I kind of came to, I saw SHE was beside me and what an

anxious look was on HER face! I wanted to tell HER, 'it's okay', but all I could do was wag feebly.

"Don't leave me, Abbi. Not yet. Not now," SHE said, and I saw tears in HER eyes with my one good one, just before the vision faded.

I knew I had to leave. SHE had given me a forever home, but now I was going to my forever and ever home.

I was ready.

SHE will be coming soon, I know, as SHE kisses me on the top of my head. I hope SHE leaves the lipstick mark, like always, that SHE later has to wash away. It always felt so good, the cool water in my hair, like a benediction.

I'm off now. As the wise man said, we are only here for a visit. My visit is ending. I feel it. HER's will be over soon, and SHE will join me. I told you. SHE and I are sisters under the skin.

Ah, there. There is the light. I am coming. I can tell.

I am almost home.

AFTERTHOUGHT

What Abbi gave me, what she brought to my life?

It is immeasurable.

I can live better because of her.

I am eternally grateful to her – to have had that sweet little heartbeat in my house – to have caressed her curly hair - to have cuddled with her warmth and love – and best of all, to know I will soon enough be able to tousle her fluffy fur once again in our forever and ever home.

Until we are reunited, I feel Abbi is still with me. Her bed is still on the red couch. Her leash rests on top of the clothes dryer in the laundry room, and I have a picture of her little snaggle-toothed face on the side table next to my bed. It helps.

I love you, little dog. May you finally rest in peace.

If this seems sentimental, it is, but it is MY truth.

EPILOGUE

"Abbi's Forever Home" is written in part because the cruelty towards our companion animals evinced across the United States is so disturbing.

There are many instances of maltreatment: puppy mills being the worst; inhumane chaining outside of dogs in inclement weather; the lack of medical care in certain shelters where flea infestations, the debilitating disease Parvo, and rotting teeth are common in the inmates; the dog-fighting game where animals are brutally trained to kill; violence against domestic animals in homes; early euthanasia.

The list goes on.

"Abbi's Forever Home" is a work of recognition of the enormous gift an older dog can bring to the life of an elderly person. In shelters across the country, the aging animals sit in cages waiting the inevitable. What a waste, when each could provide a loving presence to a lonely old person.

I have had dogs for my entire life, from Labradors, Poodles, Cocker Spaniels, mutts, to rescue dogs, the latter being the most personally rewarding.

Involved with The Bide-A-Wee Home Association, a no-kill shelter, with facilities in New York City, Wantagh and Westhampton, Long Island, for over 30 years, I was a board member, then held the position of secretary, and for the last 10 years of my tenure, chairman of the board.

The welfare of the residents of the shelter complex was paramount. Raising money, seeing that excellent veterinary care both in-house and available to the public was provided, instrumental in building a retirement home for elderly animals, all these were the responsibility of the board of directors.

A series of Galas at the Plaza Hotel and The Pierre in New York City, were held over a number of years, where dogs were featured guests – the cadaver dogs during 911, police dogs of great valor, therapy dogs, seeing eye dogs – much to the delight and generosity of the attendees.

I write "Abbi's Forever Home" at the age of 92. It tells the tale (no pun intended) of my latest dear companion, a toy poodle named Abbi. It is told from the little dog's point of view, an 11-year-old, half-blind, puppy mill graduate. The book is a memoir for two – an elderly woman and an aging dog who form an intense bond of love for one another in their golden years.

It can happen. It did for me.

.

Printed in the United States
By Bookmasters

This is the poignant story of the bond created between a ninety-two-year-old widow who lives alone and an eleven-year-old toy poodle, with one good eye, who is a graduate of a puppy mill. Told in the little dog's voice, it depicts the love and solace they find together and the value of adopting an aging pet to share one's golden years.

Elizabeth Cooke was a member of the board of directors of The Bide-A-Wee Home Association in New York, a no-kill animal shelter complex, for over 30 years. The last ten years of her tenure, she served as chairman of the board. She has been an animal activist her whole life.

www.elizabethcookebooks.com

U.S. $8.99

ISBN 978-1-4582-2166-7

COVER GRAPHICS/ART CREDIT BY:
TODD ENGEL

5089

9 781458 221667

Yudit Maros

Apple of My I
The Four Practices of Self-Love

Tools for authentic living in a chaotic world